Glacier
National Park

by Mike Graf

Consultant:
Steve Dodd, Director
Park Ranger Training Program
Northern Arizona University
Flagstaff, Arizona

Bridgestone Books
an imprint of Capstone Press
Mankato, Minnesota

Bridgestone Books are published by Capstone Press
151 Good Counsel Drive, P.O. Box 669, Mankato, Minnesota 56002
http://www.capstone-press.com

Library of Congress Cataloging-in-Publication Data
Graf, Mike.
  Glacier National Park / by Mike Graf.
  p. cm.—(National parks)
  Includes bibliographical references (p. 23) and index.
  Summary: Describes Glacier National Park, including its location, history, plants and
animals, weather, and activities for visitors.
  ISBN 0-7368-2220-8 (hardcover)
  1. Glacier National Park (Mont.)—Juvenile literature. [1. Glacier National Park (Mont.)
2. National parks and reserves.] I. Title
F737 .G5G64 2004
917.86'52—dc21   2002154605

Editorial Credits
Christianne C. Jones, editor; Linda Clavel, series designer; Enoch Peterson, book designer;
  Anne McMullen, illustrator; Alta Schaffer, photo researcher; Karen Risch, product
  planning editor

Photo Credits
Cheryl R. Richter, 4, 16
Jeff Henry/Roche Jaune Pictures, Inc., 10, 14, 18
John Elk III, cover, 1, 17
Library of Congress, 8
Tom & Pat Leeson, 12
Tom Till, 6

1 2 3 4 5 6 08 07 06 05 04 03

Table of Contents

Montana

Glacier National Park

Beauty abounds in Glacier National Park. The park has hundreds of lakes, thousands of waterfalls, and more than 700 miles (1,127 kilometers) of hiking trails. Valleys and mountains cover the land. A variety of plants and animals live in the park.

Glacier National Park is in northern Montana. The park covers more than 1 million acres (400,000 hectares) of land. It is larger than the state of Rhode Island.

Canada's Waterton Lakes National Park and Glacier National Park share the border between the United States and Canada. Together, the two parks make up an International Peace Park.

In 1910, the U.S. government set aside land to make Glacier National Park. It became the country's tenth national park. More than 1.5 million people visit Glacier National Park every year.

Running Eagle Falls is one of the thousands of waterfalls in Glacier National Park.

Glacier National Park's mountains, valleys, and lakes formed over millions of years. Water once covered the land. Rock and soil under the water slowly hardened into thick layers of limestone, mudstone, and sandstone.

About 60 million years ago, Earth's crust began to shift. The rock layers began to crack and break. One rock plate slid over another rock plate. The rocks piled up to create mountains.

Glaciers helped shape the park's land. These slow-moving sheets of ice and snow slid over the land. They carved deep valleys. Some of the valleys filled with melted ice from the glaciers. Water-filled valleys turned into lakes.

Glaciers also changed the color of some lakes in the park. As glaciers moved, they turned rocks into powder. The powder fell into some of the lakes. The powder turned the lakes turquoise.

Glaciers carved the valleys and the mountains that form Glacier National Park.

8

People in Glacier

American Indians have lived in Glacier National Park for more than 10,000 years. The Blackfeet, the Kalispel, the Kootenai, the Salish, and the Flathead were all early residents of the area. The Blackfeet controlled most of the land.

American Indian influences are still shown throughout the park. Stoney Indian Pass is named after American Indians. Chief Mountain is a sacred place for the Blackfeet. Many American Indian reservations are located near the park.

European Americans came to the area in the 1800s. David Thompson was the first European American to record what he saw at Glacier.

In 1885, naturalist George Bird Grinnell came to the Glacier area. He asked the government to protect it. In 1910, President William Howard Taft signed a bill to create Glacier National Park.

George Bird Grinnell called Glacier National Park "The Crown of the Continent."

Weather

The weather is different on each side of Glacier National Park. The western side receives the most precipitation. The eastern side of the park is drier, windier, and sunnier.

Weather at Glacier National Park changes quickly. A warm summer day often turns cool and rainy in the afternoon. Snow can fall anytime. In August of 1992, a foot of snow fell on the northeastern corner of the park.

Winters at Glacier are long and cold. Winter temperatures average between 20 and 40 degrees Fahrenheit (minus 7 and 4 degrees Celsius). Mountain peaks are almost always covered in snow.

Summer weather brings many tourists to Glacier National Park. Summer temperatures in the lower areas of the park are about 70 to 80 degrees Fahrenheit (21 to 27 degrees Celsius). It is usually 10 to 15 degrees cooler in the mountains.

Glacier National Park gets an average annual snowfall of 138 inches (351 centimeters).

Plants

Glacier National Park's colorful wildflower display and thick forests cover the land. Visitors see a large variety of plants while hiking through the park.

More than 1,800 different kinds of plants grow in the park. Heather, violets, and glacier lilies are some of the flowers that bloom in the mountains. Indian paintbrush, asters, and shooting stars bloom in the valleys.

Thick, green forests cover most of Glacier. The park has 25 different types of trees. Evergreen trees cover almost two-thirds of the park. Spruce, fir, and lodgepole pine trees grow in the park. Large western red cedar trees and hemlock trees are other common trees in Glacier.

Many trees grow just below Glacier's highest peaks. These trees include subalpine firs, pines, and Engelmann spruce. But trees do not grow above the tree line. The tree line is the highest point trees can grow on a mountain because of the weather.

In the summer, wildflowers and grass cover the slopes and valleys in Glacier National Park.

Animals

People come to Glacier National Park to see the wildlife. Mountain goats, bighorn sheep, and moose roam the area. Visitors sometimes spot gray wolves. The gray wolf is endangered. It is one of the many protected animals in the park.

Vistors might also see grizzly bears. More grizzlies live in Glacier than in any other place in the United States, except Alaska. More than 300 grizzly bears make the park their home.

Many birds fly around Glacier's mountains, lakes, and streams. Ospreys, golden eagles, and harlequin ducks are common. Bald eagles also live in the park.

Glacier National Park is home to ptarmigans as well. These birds are brown in the summer and white in the winter. This color change helps them match their surroundings. It hides them from predators.

Mountain goats shed their coats every year.

A variety of activities are available at Glacier National Park. Some people enjoy kayaking and boating. Others enjoy fishing. Most park visitors drive on the scenic Going-to-the-Sun Road. This road winds into the mountains and along steep cliffs.

Many people enjoy hiking in Glacier National Park. They walk along more than 700 miles (1,127 kilometers) of trails. Short and long hiking trails wind through the park. Hidden Lake Trail is one of the most popular trails.

Safety

Visitors need to be careful while hiking. Hikers should always follow the marked trails or stay with a guide. They should also stay in groups.

Black bears and grizzly bears can be dangerous. Rangers tell people to make noise by clapping or singing while hiking. This warns the bears that people are coming.

The water in Glacier's streams and rivers is fast and cold. Rocks near these streams can be slippery. Hikers need to be aware of these conditions.

Park Issues

Glacier National Park is named for the glaciers that created the park's scenery. These glaciers are melting because of climate changes. In 1850, the park had about 150 glaciers. Only about 40 glaciers are left. Some people believe that all the glaciers in the park will melt in the next 20 to 30 years.

Some people think the climate change is due to global warming. Global warming means the temperature of Earth's atmosphere is rising. This change happens when pollution gets into the atmosphere, trapping the sun's heat. Other people believe the climate change is a natural event.

The park's plants and animals are affected by the climate change. The plants and animals may not be able to adjust to the temperature change. Plants are disappearing, and animals are leaving. Despite these changes, Glacier National Park is still a wonderful place to visit.

About 40 glaciers remain in Glacier National Park today.

Map Key

0 5 10 Kilometers

0 5 10 Miles

△ Campsite

◎ Glacier

----- Hiking Trail

⋀ Mountain Peak

▦ Park Area

🚹 Park Visitor Center

▒▒▒ Railroad

━━ Road

〰 Waterfall

Waterton Lakes National Park

Canada

United States

Apassiz Glacier

Rainbow Glacier

Stoney Indian Pass

Chief Mountain

Quartz Creek

Grinnell Glacier

St. Mary Visitor Center

St. Mary Lake

Longfellow Peak

Lake McDonald Falls

Going-to-the-Sun Road

Hidden Lake

St. Mary Falls

Going-to-the-Sun Road

Lake McDonald

Park Headquarters

Loneman Mountain

Twin Falls

Two Medicine Lake

Lake Isabel

Map Activity

Glacier National Park has many trails. Look at the trails on the map. Also notice some of Glacier's scenic places named on the map. See how far it is to hike from one place to another in the park.

What You Need
Ruler
20-inch (50-centimeter) piece of string

What You Do
1. Find the beginning of a trail on the map. Pick a spot to hike to from that trail.
2. Using the ruler, measure the distance from the beginning of the trail to your destination. Use the map's scale to find out how far this distance is in miles or kilometers.
3. Now measure the distance you have to hike. Place one end of the string at the beginning of the trail. Then lay the string down, following the winding path of the trail until you reach your site.
4. Measure the length of string you used. Use the scale to find the distance in miles or kilometers. Try this activity with several trails on the map.

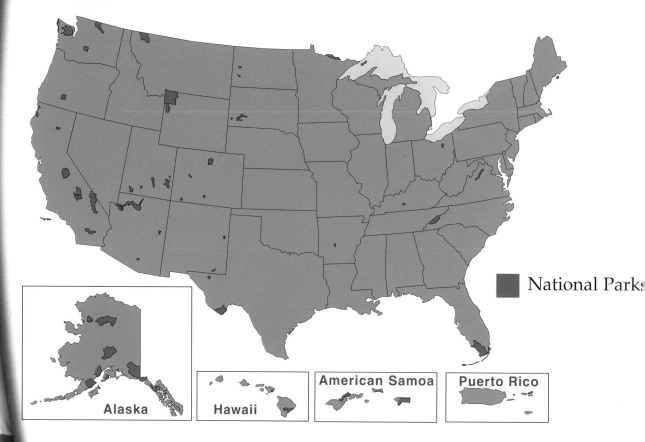

National Parks

About National Parks

In 1916, the U.S. government formed the National Park Service. This group was created to oversee all U.S. park lands. The U.S. government creates national parks to protect natural areas. People can camp, hike, and view the wildlife and scenery. But they are not allowed to hunt or build on park lands. Today, the United States has more than 50 national parks.

Words to Know

endangered (en-DAYN-jurd)—at risk of dying out

glacier (GLAY-shur)—a slow-moving sheet of ice and snow

global warming (GLOH-buhl WOR-ming)—the gradual temperature rise of the Earth's atmosphere

naturalist (NACH-ur-uh-list)—someone who studies animals and plants

plates (PLAYTSS)—large sheets of rock that make up Earth's crust

precipitation (pre-sip-i-TAY-shuhn)—the snow and rain an area receives

subalpine (sub-AL-pine)—consisting of plant life that lives just below the tree line in mountainous and northern areas

tree line (TREE LINE)—the point on a mountain where trees can no longer grow because of weather conditions

Read More

Petersen, David. *National Parks.* A True Book. New York: Children's Press, 2001.

Raatma, Lucia. *Our National Parks.* Let's See. Minneapolis: Compass Point Books, 2002.

Sateren, Shelley Swanson. *Montana Facts and Symbols.* The States and Their Symbols. Mankato, Minn.: Capstone Press, 2003.

Useful Addresses

Glacier National Park
Park Headquarters
West Glacier, MT 59936

National Park Service
1849 C Street NW
Washington, DC 20240

Internet Sites

Do you want to find out more about Glacier National Park?
Let FactHound, our fact-finding hound dog,
do the research for you.

Here's how:
1) Visit **http://www.facthound.com**
2) Type in the **Book ID** number: **0736822208**
3) Click on **FETCH IT**.

FactHound will fetch Internet sites picked
by our editors just for you!

Index